I am fine:
don't read th

Steve Anc

Author of the wounded butterfly

Published by Prolific Pulse Press LLC

Lisa Tomey-Zonneveld, Manager prolficpulse@gmail.com

Library of Congress Control Number: 2022913932

ISBN 979-8-9863237-5-6 Paperback

ISBN 979-8-9863237-6-3 Digital

Cover Photography Source: Wonderlane on Unsplash

Author's social media information
Website: www.ancpoems.com
Facebook page: https://www.facebook.com/ancspoem
Twitter: https://twitter.com/steveanc

For permission requests, write to the author at

Email: stvanc@gmail.com

Table of Contents

Dedication

To my father (the late Mr. Ajuzie Nwaorisara) who death plugged before poetry picked me.

To my mother (Mrs. Nwaorisara Ihemamma) whose prayers keep me going.

To Mark Rasmussen, whose contribution I will keep at heart.

To Florence Rasmussen, whose remarkable rules keep me moving.

Previously Published Books by Steve Anc

I wrote this for you

The filthy hands and other poems

The children of none: read the power of simple words

What the ant saw: read a poem and thirst for two

The untold truth about love, sex, and friendship

Acknowledgments

Lisa Combs Otto, a beautiful soul I so much admire and whose poem I can't stop reading.

Lisa Tomey-Zonneveld, whose support I cannot take for granted.

To Dr. Val Karanxha whose support and encouragement I can't deny.

To Ezeakunne Henry for firstly recognizing me as an international writer.

Jason Cook, for your review.

Katina Woodruff Borgerson, for your review.

Max Speed, for your review.

My siblings, you guys are amazing, don't

forget.

All the wounded souls in search of solace.

All those who think they are alone.

Those that place self-care above everything.

The readers, who look up at the moon and make a wish.

Those creatures who inspired each poem but can't read it.

About The Book

Here is a book that leaves a footprint on the heart. I am fine: don't read this poem is one of those deep, sad, and metaphorical poetic books that are supposed to be read with unbroken concentration. Cleverly, each poem introduces answers to lots of ever-asked questions on peace, mental health, humanity, and self-love and the poet (Steve Anc) had you in mind during the entire writing process.

I am fine: don't read this poem is filled with broken pieces, ugly truth, and lots of lines for those that have been mentally misunderstood. The mood of some poems becomes much darker more intense and hard-hitting as you read.

This book can also serve as peace for many souls, strength for the fading eyes, and self-care for the forgotten.

Book Reviews

Florence Rasmussen, a poet, United Kingdom

This book of poetry is different from Steve Anc's previous collections. This is his finest collection up to date. He is challenging the reader to face some hard truths about the abuse and suffering of the disenfranchised poor and to look at their own often denied mental health issues, but this is not a book of mournful angst. There is love, hopefulness, and joy, along with conversations with kinsmen, his mother, and God that show the poet has come through his trials. There is indeed something for all awaiting the reader.

And of course, written in Steve's unique style, he writings always has a strong ethereal spiritual essence which is a mirroring of his personality.

POEM DESCRIPTION

I am fine: don't read this poem

This poem is my favorite poem in this collection. It has given me cause, though. I want the narrator to be not just one person but an amalgam of several, otherwise, there seems to be too much pain suffered by one person. For me, it is the epitome of the internal thoughts and feelings of unworthiness felt by sufferers of depressive illness. If the reader was in any doubt about the theme of this collection this piece can leave the reader in no doubt. The title alone draws the reader's eye, it indicates the narrator doesn't want the responsibility of depressing the reader, yet still wants to show that he is not fine but also wants his state of mind understood.

It has been written in a short line format that acts like bullet points initially emphasizing why the reader should not read the piece as in: *You don't have to stress the eyes Cos you won't understand* followed by *You could be caged in.* and further please to not read, which reveal more about how he is feeling himself and about himself.

When we reach *I said stop* the mood of this poem becomes much darker more intense and hard-hitting. We see a litany of bad experiences suffered by the narrator laid bare in black and white. There can be no shrinking away from this hard truth. Following this, the poem moves to a softer emotion: *life is funny* here we are witnessing an acceptance of what has gone before. The narrator is telling the reader not to worry about him reiterating that he is fine, but just who is he trying to convince? The very end of the poem shows how emotionally draining the experience has been, maybe the poet is talking about the actual writing of this piece as much as experiencing depression firsthand, as seen in: *I need rest, Please, leave me in the dark* adds to the feeling that all is not well.

I am somebody

I know you have a surname

Because it was written with bliss and care

But the letters on mine were incomplete

Because the winds and storms displaced a lot

And my birth history read as an illusion

In this poem, the author has drawn on personal experience to bring attention to all disadvantaged children whether displaced by war, natural forces, or just by dint of birth.

We see this in the first line: *I know you have a surname* And then later in: *Cos the walls and the gates need a complete name.* Also, a space for parents reminds the reader that education is still not available for all, causing many to miss out on receiving a longed-for education.

This is not a tale of woe. The narrator's voice is strong and deviant he will not be defined by his past. As seen in the whole of the third stanza, each line starts with *I care not* and ends with a determined even stronger voice in the final stanza, as he declares I will and finally the strong statement: *Because I am somebody.*

The thorn in the tongue

You said the light would come back just as darkness did, this is a metaphor for darkness of the mind and thoughts being spoken of. The opening two couplets use a clever play on the same or linked words as in- 'light' and 'bright' not only linked by the rhyme they also belong to the same lexicon but are used to infer light and darkness.

The following stanzas are used to drive home the experience of depression: In stanza three *It came with compartments* cleverly shows the intricacies of mental illness, compartmentalizing is a mental Chinese puzzle box, by using three different images on three lines the author is ensuring his readers understand what he is saying.

The final stanza is dealing with the relentless nature of depressive illness even after admitting he has problems the natator finds no peace *Even after I migrated from silence to tears.*

※

A note to my kinsmen

This poem will resonate with anybody far from their place of birth or their family. The beginning line is a direct plea to the narrator's kinsmen. *Could you please the silence* he is begging them to stop his thoughts in the night.

The body of the poem shows the narrator is missing all that he holds dear and is homesick for the old familiar life and values. We see this in the whole of the second and third stanzas *I have not forgotten the road that paved my path* to *Even the glamorous radiance of the moon at twilight* despite the sparsity of descriptive detail, each line triggers a different memory snapshot.

The final stanza is an explanation as to why he has not forgotten his roots *Because…I have not gone with the magnificent roses* is telling his kinsmen and the reader that he has not been swayed by city life and ending with a declaration: *I am still the frozen conservative soul.*

What if tomorrow comes

At face value, this poem looks to be a message to another person as it is written in the third person. starting with a strong plea: *Don't you cry damn you, don't cry.* And could easily apply to every reader in some way or another at a point in their lives. In the context of this book, this poem is a message directed back at the narrator/author. Stanza one says to stop worrying about what could be evidenced in the last line *And let the calculated pain pour away.*

Stanza two: Here we read a very lyrically put the advice to break out of the bitter tears, he needs to action his success *Rather prepare your net.*

Stanza three: A warning about it will feel like an army of failures and set back that will appear. The poet uses personification to enhance the intensity of the message. *But distance yourself from the dark chap* and finishing with a reminder to prepare for all hindrances *And pile up your pyramid high.*

The fourth stanza gives two positive messages: prepare yourself for success not for failure: *Not with slashes and starkly stern, But with anticipation and enchanted sing.*

Do not cry, damn you! Don't cry! At the beginning of the fifth and final stanza reminds the reader of the narrator's first words, and the premise of the poem- to advise the narrator to keep the will to carry on living, not give up when trials come their way or let depression at lack of progress bring them down. And finishes on a positive note hinting at we never know when success is waiting around the next corner or in this case…

Review

Jason Cook, a poet, coder, United States of America

The author in progress, Steve Anc has done it again.

I am fine: don't read this poem is yet another wonderful collection of short pieces of poetry that convey deep soul and wisdom wrapped in an enigma.

It almost feels as if he is speaking directly to the ails of the heart and mind.

There is silver spilled upon his pages, and the book would do well gilt in glory.

You'd almost think he had gorged the Philosopher's stone into his very being.

A worthy addition to any library of works.

I am fine: don't read this poem

She is STRONG, but she is TIRED

She got a glimpse of her might during her childhood.

She brought a heart to get her through.

She fought for a path to keep the mark.

She sent all raining hells beneath her feet.

And she planted all beds with silk roses.

She frightened the finch and scared the sparrow.

She paved a path in the forbidden forest.

She made a metallic sword for souls to wonder about.

She made the sword gleams like the eyes of the gods...

She gave the sword power to glitter like crystal,

And make the shallow water beneath warm.

She made her intention known to all.

And her plain wish was to fix the world—

To stand at the gap between the gods and men.

To serve as the pitcher that refreshes the thirsty.

To serve as a cure-all to the wounded heart.

But her strength had sapped from within,

And no one knows she was tired.

Please tell the rainbow

Seek not to solace in faces,

Because it comes with bags of distress;

And hurries the heart to the grave.

Though man lifts man.

You will say!

But man limits man

I have seen.

Though man makes man.

I believe!

But man mars man

 You have seen!

Please in a time of distress,

Clench at the rainbow.

She sits atop the cloudy rain.

She comes atop a messy sky.

She knows when the thunderous hands clap;

She knows when the din didn't chime.

She appears betwixt the galaxy

To shoulder and pick our grumbling.

Let her carry the load,

Because she sits with the Infinite.

But she didn't steal the sky,

And she didn't drag with the moon;

She only appears to listen

Because her hands stroll through the universe.

Poetry is alive

Do not stand at the grave and weep
Ah, souls!
There is no death in poetry.
Cos the sea could not drum without poetry
The sea birds could not swim without poetry.
Stars could not be praised without poetry.

Without poetry, the stars quake, and the moon quivers.
Without poetry, the earth lost its beauty.
And without poetry death laud itself.

Yet, let us reason along:
If poetry is dead the birds could not sing.
If poetry is dead the moon could not dance.
If poetry is dead the rainbow could not spread.
If poetry is death the sky could not be appreciated.
If poetry is dead, today would never exist.
Without poetry...
There would be no butterfly
Cos butterfly signifies beauty.

The wounded butterfly

Hello Mma,
Let's measure a new skin for the world.
Let's cut off the colored and dusty parts,
And make a universal uniform for humanity.
Cos the bright skins are stained.

 Hello Mma,
Let's dig for the root of the relationship
And hold it up so high for them to see.
Let's show its exact color to the world
And make new eyes for them to see.
With new hearts for them to wear
Cos the old eyes and hearts are hazy and hardened.

Hello Mma,
Please come!
Come let's stand on the Warisan Merdeka.
Let's ask why humans conceived hatred.
Let's show them the true color of their conception,
And make new wombs for them,
Cos the previous wombs are bloody.

Hello Mma,

Please come!

Come let us unveil some feelings.

Let's unveil some scars and harms.

Let's show them the suffering of a naked heart.

Let's show them the mark of their arrows,

And make new hearts for them,

Cos the previous hearts are point to kill.

How I wooed the moon

They said none could woo the moon.

But mine was a different strategy:

I met her when her mind was open...

When she wore neither sleep nor slumber

And spoke through the holes on her skin.

They said none could talk to the moon.

But mine was a different one:

I went with flax flowers and forget me not...

When she wore a smile in a pink dress And

splashed them before her steps.

They said none could please the moon.

But mine was different:

I went to her with a slim cup...

with neither pride nor pretense,

Also, rob off my ego on my way,

And filled my gut with splashes of solemn and solace.

I am fine: don't read this poem

They finally announced noon could marry the moon.

But mine was a slim and a sincere approach:

I went to her a whole being—

When she wore her light ears and crystal eyes

And soaked into her soul from the cracks in her eyes.

Please tell my father

Please tell him that I will get there,

Though, I don't have the know-how;

But I have gotten the keen eyes

Between the mountain and the sea.

Tell my father I will remember the paths,

Though I don't know the way of the stars,

But the insight with the light will lead me

Between shining faith and glowing hope.

Tell him I won't thrust his name,

Though I have thrust challenges below the palm pine,

And I have tapped the only wine of a banter,

Between the thorns and piercing trees.

Tell my father I still wish he were here,

Though my lovely roses withered within the dream,

When the lingering bell dot rang,

Between the fairy moon and fading dream.

Between the fairy moon and fading dream.

Not all that sniff escape

I thought I would lick my lips when the feast is over.

I thought I would wear a robe after I had naked the world.

I thought I would be the best after I had broken some beings.

I thought I would drink my soup after I had poisoned the soup.

I thought I would smile after I had shamed some soul.

It has been my custom to behave without empathy.

It has been my norm to lick without caution.

It has been my policy to poison the soup.

It has been my joy to watch souls whither.

It has been my manner to nip the remaining bud.

Though caution came, I wrapped myself with narcist.

Empathy knocked, and I whacked the door at a glance.

Cause after effect looked, I responded with a heavy sigh

Because highly a hundred nights, I have seen victory.

Behold!

How sad had it all ended...

Though I wanted to happily hurry home as usual,

With comfort in my heart and hurts in their hearts;

But I had licked the soup I could not finish.

I am fine: don't read this poem

The beatitude

Beatitude is not frowsy
Her wings are wild
Her ears are light
Her thoughts are blissful
She is the grace of the morning
The peace of the stars
The marriage of the moon
The dance of the earth
She broods the world
And bruises the war

Beatitude
The force of gratitude
The beam of the sunbeam
Like the line of learning
Deep underneath deep
The cause of remembrance
The meaning of being
The walk of self
Out of pseudo stem
And out of slumber

I am fine: don't read this poem

Beatitude

The declaration of blessedness

The kiss of loveliness

The stretch of beautification

Solemn and ecstasy

The poster of peace

The pioneer of heavenly truce

Undaunted and calm

In beautiful notion

Beatitude...

The unhealed child in us

From the scene of childhood memory, I come,
As I could hear the drum of my faults afar:
Playing the beat of shortcomings.
Blowing the flute of my stubbornness.
Even the sorry I didn't whisper when I should.

The fight I caused without a fault, it recalled.
The bullies that I bought with my only coin, it recollected.
The lies that caused others pain, it remembered

Though it is playing the beat of up to the hill,
But am here with empathy and compassion;
In search of a therapist that could heal the unhealed child in me.

I am fine: don't read this poem

You don't have to see this:

You don't have to stress the eyes

Cos you won't understand

Yes!

You would not

You don't have to...

Nothing is wrong!

You don't have to read my poem

You will wither into my pain

Please don't read these lines

You could be caged.

Please don't go further

Tears may freely roll

Eyes may freely swell

Hearts may easily bleed

If you continue with this write

It may read the truth

Yes!

I said stop!

I have been accused

I have been depressed

I have been blamed

I am fine: don't read this poem

I have been chained

I have been bullied

Raped

Ignored

Used

Betrayed

Mostly for zero cause

I can feel your concern

Yes!

I can!

But you should not...

Life is funny

And I have seen it

You don't have to see that

You don't have to think that

Cos nothing is wrong

Do not worry

Do not think it

Do not stress it

I am fine

Forget the allegations

Forget the interrogations

Forget the accusation

I am fine: don't read this poem

I mean forget the...
I am fine
Nothing is wrong
Just let me be
I need to be alone
I need peace
I need rest
Please, leave me in the dark
I am fi...

What I left unsaid when it was boiling

I wonder if abusive souls
    Are always happy?
I wonder if their stream of words
    Had cleaned their homes?
Did they sing with happy harmony?
When the lake is calm?
Or did they sink into regret
  When the battle is over?

I wonder if a loose tongue
    Jiggles with enjoyment?
I wonder if the gossiping souls
 purchase piles of time for retrospection?

 As their words dance on a highland wind,
Scattering the bricks that built souls,
Did they sieve their muckle phrases?
Bite their bitter pills
And think of the act of their venoms?

I am fine: don't read this poem

I am somebody

I know you have a surname
Because it was written with bliss and care
But the letters on mine were incomplete
Because the winds and storms displaced a lot
And my birth history read as an illusion

Alas, is my wish to see the wall of the schools
But I couldn't see the gates of the schools
Cos the walls and the gates need a complete name
Also, a space for parental signatures

But I care not why mine was not complete
I care not why the history wasn't there
I care not who hides the registrar's slip
I care not who took the remaining pen
I care not who left a note with the piteous sigh

I will pierce the heart of history
I will bridge the gap between the schools
And write my complete name on the same book
Because I am somebody!

My prayers: points from poetic perspective

Oh, Creator!

Bless souls of gentle birth.

Bake kindness for the kind-hearted.

Advocate protection to the crushed.

Blow a trumpet-like breakthrough to the broken.

And lift many from crimson menacing flames.

Bless men of gentle spirit,

May your high hands elevate them

With constant light and dynamite,

That their grains may multiply,

And their supply may be more.

Reach out to the starving children,

Stitch up their tattered bellies.

Reach out to the willing hearts,

Give strength to their dragging feet.

Round diligent heads with stable crowns

And bless their shores with clean sea.

The Children of the moon

They picked all the eleven children,

And made some characters out of their creations:

They made two became doctors,

and gave them separate pairs of the stethoscope.

And turned one into a psychologist,

gave him a weird instinct to pick up sounds.

Made one political activist,

and hung honorable on his sleeves.

Made one a businessman,

and called him the boss of all bosses.

Lubricated one with the ointment of the pope.

Toss one-off as a forsaken dice.

Cut one's trousers to dress as an imam,

and deposited Arabic in his bank of knowledge.

They thought one was a criminal,

and suspected every action he took.

Made one fell in love with the wrong soul

and washed her withered in depression.

Detached the remaining one from her positive energy.

That is why the moon lacks children till today!

Why I learned French

When I was on French land
The rhymes on their tunes made me learn some words
But some pronunciation is odd
Some come with a skinny structure
A few too large to absorb
Others in an SVO manner

Nevertheless, I love how friends became ami
And how travel turned into voyager
But some words don't travel so well
Because they called their road route
And the bent vehicle to voiture
Swerved car park to le s
Stationnement
Turned cities into Ville
And twisted a house to Maison

I smiled as I saw cloth turned to chiffon
And waited when I heard puissance as power
Had a rethink when I learned women as femme

I am fine: don't read this poem

Question my instinct as I read man as homme
And smiled when a happy child was called
enfant
Mais, la beauté c'est la
If you ask for direction there
Remember that there is là
And the street is known as la rue
Places were given as plās
And numéro de Maison drawn house number
Bienvenue took the place of welcome

The Love we brought

See solemnly sing the bird, and gently dance the trees

Singing the amazing wishing day is here,

Pointing at the face that owns the day

Calling to all the voices to wishfully whisper the song

Showing him the love they brought

Wrapped with awesome words and stunning wisdom

To fence his face with laughter and comfort

As he rambles with scents breath of birth

We don't have the strength

There are twenty-four ribs

And two hundred and six bones in us,

But some bones are broken by problems.

Some veins are pressed by pressures.

Some arteries lack tunica,

Other with lesser elastic fibers.

Remember that some blood cells are red,

Some cells have white coats

And others wear platelets,

But some tissues had been eaten up by ailment,

And some minds are eaten up by burden.

Do not assume that souls could stand the push,

Cos people are not as strong as you thought.

And some intestines are hungry, and feet lack strength.

Do not slam a soul out of anger

And do not assume he could stand the blast

Cos only a hit could die a soul.

Everything will be fine

Oh, how I love the laughing sky
As it slips and matches the darkest tunnel
Knifing and splintering the cloudy rays
Stitching and fastening the thundered rock
With the threads of possibilities trends

High o'er the hill I first lay my heart,
Expecting when the moon will cheer up the night,
As I stare and stare for the crystal stars
And glance for glamour glimpse of mortal grace.

Though, sometimes bewitched beneath the moon
Co' no mortal man could feel the demon awake
But still, still, I heard the breeze refrain
If your glamorous songs aim at the stars
Then everything will be fine

The note I left for my kinsmen

Could you please silence the darkness?
And gift the light the right to shine
Because I have not forgotten my root:

I have not forgotten the road that paved my path.
I have not ignored the net that sieved my grains.
I have not defied the river that cleaned my feet.
I have not bypassed the lad that married stammering,
Even the tender tears that he shed…

I have not forgotten the laughing dove on the riverbank.
I have not ignored the woody stork that blinks by the side.
I have not excluded the dusty bench betwixt the town.
I have not forgotten the sipping cup with ancestral sage,
Even the glamorous radiance of the moon at twilight…

Because …
I have not gone with the magnificent roses,
Neither with the stunning gleams
Nor with the swift ride of pleasant tides,
I am still the frozen conservative soul.

Page 18

...and after page 17,
the breeze opened a page:

Where all monsters were stocked,
And masters were reserved.

A page where all good hearts were published,
And beautiful souls long for the butterflies.

Where freedom purchased her name,
And parental discipline sounds not.

Where youthful voices sing so loud,
And mundane hit the drum.

Where decent souls press for the mark,
And gifted runners roll for a tag.

Where singers crave lyrics,
With faith mouth and hopeful eyes.

I am fine: don't read this poem

Where hearts cherish a bunch of frivolities
And purchase deaf ears for their souls.

It is where some hearts are lightened forever,
And some souls married the prison,
Because ignorance clenched against the sky!
Because ignorance clenched against the sky!

The magick November 5th

Since men were made for remembrance
And nature was made to set laws
Let's tap at the magick on November 5th
And remember the awesome 51st year.

Let's adore a magick woman with a poetry mind
Cos none of her pieces could bore us
And her magick doesn't wear off
Even when behold with sleepy eyes.

Sometimes, I gasp with dazzling teeth
Smile from cheek to cheek
Not as a confounded creature
But as a lover of the moon
And guidance of the wild children
Cos with her works, I cut my glimpse

I am fine: don't read this poem

...but I have a poem to write

We have no aspiration for time-wasting.

We have no plan to sit on the fence.

We wish to stitch in time and stitch on time.

But we had carefully plucked off each day

Procrastinated it from root to leaves

And deposited its remains in a utopian community.

We even blamed times and seasons,

Asked why nature didn't release much of them.

We yelled at the stars and banged at the moon.

We frowned at the aquatic creatures and the ocean,

For captivating us with their beauty.

Accused the galaxies of their elegant radiance.

Slammed at the sun for its shortcomings,

But scented selves with the ornament of saints.

Why I love nature and the moon

I am a lad with a slim heart,
Littered with positive current
And greased with a free spirit,
C0s' I could feel the ground beneath my feet.

I am a soul with empathy.
I have seen that softness is not weakness,
Cos the moon loves a soft soul,
And it takes love to cherish the sea.

I could feel the breath of the moon,
Not with my slim heart anymore.
I could hear the voice of nature,
Neither with my clustered mind
Cos the heart and mind might forget.

But I could feel with my soul,
And I could hear with my spirit
Cos my soul neither fail nor forget.

In search of solace

Aye!
See...
As the space spread with no limit
And the sun stretches from the orbit
Yet our earth only boils and growls
With countless constellations cast
Please search space for solace

Just think!
Think...
As the sea stretches as a happy child
And a thousand grains of sand that swim
Yet humanity crams the sea
With countless waste and spoil
Rinse the seashore and build stories
Still, search that space for solace

Just look!
Look...
As the galaxies smile with full cheek
And the face of a happy sun
Yet humans hug sadness
With a lot of complaints and injustice
Please search space for solace

A letter to the man on the sixth floor

My only medal is the spit on my pen
Sometimes, it floods...
To win me shelter, shoes, and food.
Another time, it rains...
To appease the children of the moon
And kill the wing of injustice.

Lots had gained glaring gleam medals
Proudly won in the fearless fights
Cause life garnishes colorful gleam
With beautiful crosses that bravely shine
Though their heart quest not behind the floor

But life quietly quickens my heart to quest:
It left me a letter to leave.
A letter to unwrap and rewrite
A letter to send to the sixth floor:
To quest for the sound beneath the beat
To quest for a season without breath
But God's good mercy speak

...on the 8th day

...and on the 8th day
 I saw a sad impromptu knowledge
jumped into the depth of the Oji River
With the gathered content from the womb
To dump its sea of generational notions.

From birth, we move as a timeless breeze,
Welcome each thought as a wild paradise.
Think neither thought, a doom, nor action, a risk.
Know not fire, a burn, nor sea, a deep,
With broad lips and no secret, a keep,
And shamed the angel of the chilling soul.

That was the lapses of being a child.
The lapses the young deities discussed:
When the old war-gods held up their heads,
With laws of forms and meters of low tones,
Within a calendar of eighth hours and eighth days.

Where is humility

On being asked, "where is humility?"

My heart yearned for a soul:
A sincere soul with a piece of empathy.
His soulful thoughts piece our solitude,
Spreading proverbs as leafless booms

On being asked, "where are fun and beautiful soul?"

My heart pointed to Akamo:
A county flower that dispersed his array.
The Crystal petals that brighten a sad soul,
As his charm spread from earth to sky.

On being asked, who is the Mark Foresight of Africa?"

My mind associated that with Akamo:
The inky fool!
The breath of etymologicon,
With a circular stroll into the hidden connections of the
English Language.

I am fine: don't read this poem

On being asked, "where is the soul that knows Yoruba
saying?"

I live to relate it to Akamo:
He uses the sage as a waterfall,
With the same power that softens the soil,
Pleased the desert and sluggish brook.

A tale by the man on the roadside

Set not your foot on the grave

Till you hear what the gods are saying:

There is no joy in divided tracks.

The joy that dwells in envy had expired.

The morning had chased the mourning.

And the north pole and south pole are getting married.

"Set your foot on the right track," I said.

Seek the breeze and shrub of unity

with charitable time.

 Wrap self with sublime sage.

Cos sometimes the heart speaks

Eyes thrust as confused tools

And it builds skies for misunderstanding.

Set not your foot on the grave

Till you know that...

Life is too short to waste,

How to wear the critic bite with cynic bark,

And rightly un-wrong every wrong.

I am fine: don't read this poem

Please care not to trip the dead,
Instead, rob the living with care and lively ornaments,
And only God will speed your Mark.

The Rhythm of The gods (The tale of music)

There was a man whom the gods chose to love,

A communicable man was he.

He inspired his neighbors and his neighbors admired him,

And he collected continual freedom of expression.

He pleased the sun, he dazzled the stars,

He made the dancers of the moon tilt their bottoms,

Wiped off the dusty part of the sky

And repaired the color of the sky.

He sent to hell every sad mood and waved at the birds as
they fly,

His hands were so wide and he swayed them in fantasy
ways;

And his reason was plain: easy for others to explain.

He was older than history.

He was older than the gods.

And he was higher than the hill.

He dwelt among humans, but slightly above the hill,

And windows towards the hill were accessible,

And the entrance to his compound was open—

To bring in every spark of good energy.

When he went down the street, the crowd walked with him,

Attracting, and imitating the path he trod.

I am fine: don't read this poem

He smiled at those he allured and stared at those that knew
his name,
And his name evokes beauty among other names.
His heart was so large to accommodate,
He hung his grace on his breast,
And his friends have been helpful, and he fed them with
joy,
For the happy and cheerful heart, he likes most.
Every heart had savored his soup one time or another,
And every tongue had told the mind how sweet his flavors
were.
His presence had melted the hardened heart,
And his wings had lifted the willing soul.
One day, he nibbled his little bags into holes
Little, by little, he spread his scent,
 And slowly he infected everyone,
And happiness slowly embraced all.

The storm in me

I was not created before the fall of Adam

I was not featured in the event between the serpent

I was not the pioneer of evil genius

I didn't swallow the philosopher's stone

I mean, the dark stone with a metallic ring

I was not created behind the tempest

I am not a soul with perfect knowledge

I am not a life without grief

I am not a soul without a lonely certificate

I am not that lad with zero shame

I have attended lots of lectures

I mean lectures in The School Of Difficulty

I am not a soul without misunderstanding

I have been mentally misunderstood

I have been mentally wrecked

I am not what you think I am

Cos sometimes it rages on me

But who should I tell?

Not to be tagged as a teller of tales

Cos sometimes it hits unexpectedly

Sometimes it rips me apart

I am fine: don't read this poem

Sometimes it comes like a hurricane

It comes as the wild wind

As the wind from Tarshish

You may not discern the pain

A kind that cracks my thought

You may not understand the distress

A kind you can't skin

Though, I can produce laughter

I can give out a smile

A smile with a glimpse of humor

Humor from the masquerade soul

A soul with scars and scrapes

But that is what the world admires

That is what the world sees

That is where humans live

I mean the humans of the world

A world of pretense

Where we live to show

A showcase world

I am fine: don't read this poem

Just a phase...this too will pass

I can see the sunrise from afar.
I can see the dance of the morning,
I mean, over the ten thousand distress.
I can hear a tune of change:
It is a tune worth listening to.
It is a tune worth knowing.
It is the dance of the reason.
The loveliness of the living.

I can see the first of the union from afar—
 The union betwixt hope and harmony.
I can see the light of graceful becoming.
I can feel the uniform of exploding stars—
Slaughtering the sluggish brooks
Replanting the barren deserts
I mean, replacing strength for the fragile feet.

I can see hope for the unstable soul
I can see faith in the doubtful spirit,
Maybe to nourish the shattered lips,
Or to wet the dry tongue.

I am fine: don't read this poem

I can see water for the withering roses—
I mean, the ocean for a thirsty person—
Consuming the dry days and barren nights
Replacing wilderness with healthy earth.

I can hear the voice of rain.
Alas! Run!
I can hear the sound of thunder.
Oh, run, run soul run—
I mean, to prepare your bowls and barrels:
It is the rain worth keeping.
It is the rain worth using,
Maybe to quench our grieves,
Or to spill on the lily and the iris.

What if tomorrow comes

Do not cry, damn you! Don't cry!

Silence your bitter tears,

And let the calculated pain pour away.

Rinse the sea and prepare the shore:

Prepare the mind for a pour,

And leave not the shore,

Rather prepare your net.

Sometimes discouragement marches,

It marches row upon row,

But distance yourself from the dark chap

And pile up your pyramid high.

Rinse your feet and prepare the feast,

Not with slashes and starkly stern,

But with anticipation and enchanted sing

And build a concrete wall of hope.

I am fine: don't read this poem

Do not cry, damn you! Do not cry!
Make no staircase for depression.
Make no stool for self-inflicted sufferings.
What if tomorrow comes?

A letter to my teacher

Dear sir,
I have learned to write you on this day,
And every letter was a piece of my breath.
Though, formerly dusty,
With the stitches of illiterate lines,
Known as a rant and can't of the indocile soul
But have learned to write you a letter.

Dear Sir,
 I have pierced the root of metaphor,
With the pen, I earned to earn your praise,
And every letter won't mean as it read anymore.
Though, formerly a lad with a dull intellect,
And hopeless degree,
But I have learned to write you a letter.

Dear sir,
I have learned to cave your name,
And my letters are like blossom acts—
Spreading the paths of your impact,
To make a pavement of history.

I am fine: don't read this poem

Though, not much brighter in the past,

And no stir of literate air at birth,

But from the moon, a fragment had newly clipped,

And I have learned to write you a letter.

The thorn in the tongue

You said the light would come back just as darkness did,
But I have seen the darkness that could not bright.

It is blackness with a cruel face,
A kind of blackness I could not face.

It came with compartments:
It had a series of coats with sleeves,
with lots of chambers to unleash.

It moves in a murderous manner.
It sways as King of the high throne.
It ceases not to torment.

It ceases not to mock.
It ceases not to knock.
It knocks migraine,
Even after I migrated from silence to tears.

Where that smile lies

It is in the heart of a baby
Where that smile lies.
It is in the good thought of a baby,
Where that smile lies.
It is in the giving hand of a baby,
Where that smile lies.
It is in his crystal collar,
Where that smile hangs.

Which smile do I mean?
The smile of his reigning freedom,
Caught in his dated birth.
The smile of a graceful being,
Attached on his name at birth.
The smile of a wise being,
Wired through his vein.
The smile of his birth,
Weaved on this day.

A day without sunlight

Alas!
There comes a day when all writing will slowly halt,
And the fancy written lines will read as memory.
When all hearts will admire a writing hand
As he deserts all papers and inks
And leave a spotless inspiration.

There comes a moment when all the bruises will halt.
When the world would broom the earth—
When she will wash the sea to sink her pain,
Cos the hurt mounts above the mountain.

Alas!
Let us breathe the air of now,
And pray for the face of tomorrow,
Cos all eyes would dine with death on their appointed time
When the glittering teeth slowly close.

Just keep breathing

Sometimes I sit in life as it moves,

But I can't sit on your day;

Because you are precious to me.

Remember this:

Not all storms come to disrupt your life,

Some come to align your paths.

In case I didn't tell you:

There is no secret to surviving

Just keep breathing

Just keep shining your light

Just keep being you

And it is by then your soul will split the darkest tunnel

I pray

Take these words
And the hand that writes them
Though they are handy
But they are kind and speak to the soul:

As kindness makes you beautiful,
So will greater things happen to you.
Everything you deserve
is paving away for you.

I pray...
May your soul fly so high
I pray...
May this current chapter read so loud
Louder till souls hear its volume
And may your energy speak volumes

Dear Steve

Dear Steve, it has been so long a while,
I've been on my bed wondering why,
Sometimes I fall asleep on a pile
Of your writings and awake with a sigh.

Then I sit at my table and read more,
Of the clear blue sky and the seasons,
Of the deep ocean and a poor man's tour,
Around the world searching for reasons.

Can I write this way? I wonder if,
I can never tell a story as you do.
So I pick up a pen that is not stiff,
And scribble words on a page or two.

But then I awake to a pungent smell,
Of my hair burnt by the candle flame.
How would I write when asleep I fell,
Dreaming of the hunchback of Notre Dame?

I am fine: don't read this poem

So is this what it means to create words,
About nature beauty and humanity,
About love and thrones and of mighty lords,
And how we live in society?

So tell me now dear Steve, of the rules
And how in words you paint a picture,
Of your feelings about a world so cruel,
And how you hold your pen without torture.

Till the sun goes down and rises again,
I will be here waiting to hear you give,
An account of your writing without pain,
So I could be called a poet, Dear Steve.

About the author

Steve Anc is the son of Ajuzie Nwaorisa, a Nigerian-born poet. He is a poet with searching knowledge and deep meditation on universal themes, he is quite a modern poet in his adherence to language and his use of metaphors is soul-searching.

Anc's works have been published in *Open-Door Poetry Magazine, Good Company Lit,* and *Voice from the Void.*

Poetry Soup first published "I am fine: please don't read this poem."

Anc was a contributing author in *Social Justice Inks: Anthology of Poetry*

Upon completion of this book, please write a review to post on Amazon.

Support your author today!

Support Steve Anc today!

Remember, your review could go a long way in putting a smile on my face.

Thank you!